Quoll

Christopher Cheng  Cindy Lane

WALKER BOOKS
AND SUBSIDIARIES
LONDON • BOSTON • SYDNEY • AUCKLAND

The sun is hiding behind distant hills.
The moon follows sun and soon the blue-black
sky is painted with glistening stars.

Nocturnal songs greet the moonlight.
A symphony of croaking, chirping,
creaking, scratching.

And then ...

SQUEAL

COUGH!

Quoll has woken.
It's playtime here in
the moonlit night.

Dens or shelters for Eastern Quolls can be in underground burrows, fallen hollow logs, under piles of rocks or even in buildings. They can use multiple dens that are frequently changed.

She dances once and then again with another of her kind. They play – jumping through bushes, leaping high, running across grasses, in between trees.

A pause.

A playful bite.

A breath.

A sip.

Eastern Quolls are generally solitary animals although their home ranges may overlap.

But hunger beckons, so games are done. Tonight's meal must be caught. Quoll searches around logs and sniffs beneath tree stumps.

Then she investigates inside a promising hollow but instantly darts out, chased by a growling, hungry devil searching for food too.

But she *won't* be his dinner tonight.

Feral cats and foxes are introduced predators that have preyed heavily on Eastern Quolls.

She runs towards a small mouse scurrying between bushes.

Soon it is clamped firmly between her jaws. A tiny meal for one. But Quoll has many mouths to feed.

When eating their prey Eastern Quolls will sit on their hind legs while moving their prey with their front legs.

She searches through the forest,
flashing fleet-footed, then – stops.
A distracting, twitching wallaby's
tail is a tempting plaything.

Wallaby doesn't mind at first but soon tires of Quoll and bounds away.

Eastern Quoll habitats include forests, scrub, grassland woodlands and alpine regions and especially where grasslands or farms and eucalyptus forests are close-by.

Atop a fallen tree branch, Quoll stops and stands tall sensing her surrounds.

Suddenly she bounds. Dinner is nearby.

Last night grubs were on the menu – worms and berries too. Tomorrow she will catch her own rat.

But tonight, she can sneak a little of another creature's catch. She must be quiet. Her larger carnivorous relative does not like to share.

An Eastern Quoll's diet can include small vertebrates like mice and rats, as well as birds and reptiles, and lots of insects. They are also opportunistic feeders stealing food from another predator's catch.

Quoll darts in to snatch a bite. Her cousin squeals.

A game of chasing just for two.

Quoll tires of this game and scurries off in search of her own prey. She clambers up a rock pile but slips, again and again.

Eventually she finds a steady foothold and stands tall, searching. She can sense dinner close by.

And this meal will help feed six hungry mouths.

Unlike other quolls the Eastern Quoll's hind foot has only four toes. It's missing a big toe.

Back in the nest, her young are playing,
chasing, scratching, nipping.
And grabbing.
And wrestling.

Tired, they bundle up waiting for mother, with a banquet in her jaws. When she arrives at last, the young quolls feast.

She rests.

When too large for her pouch the female Eastern Quoll will leave the young in a grass-lined den while she hunts and forages.

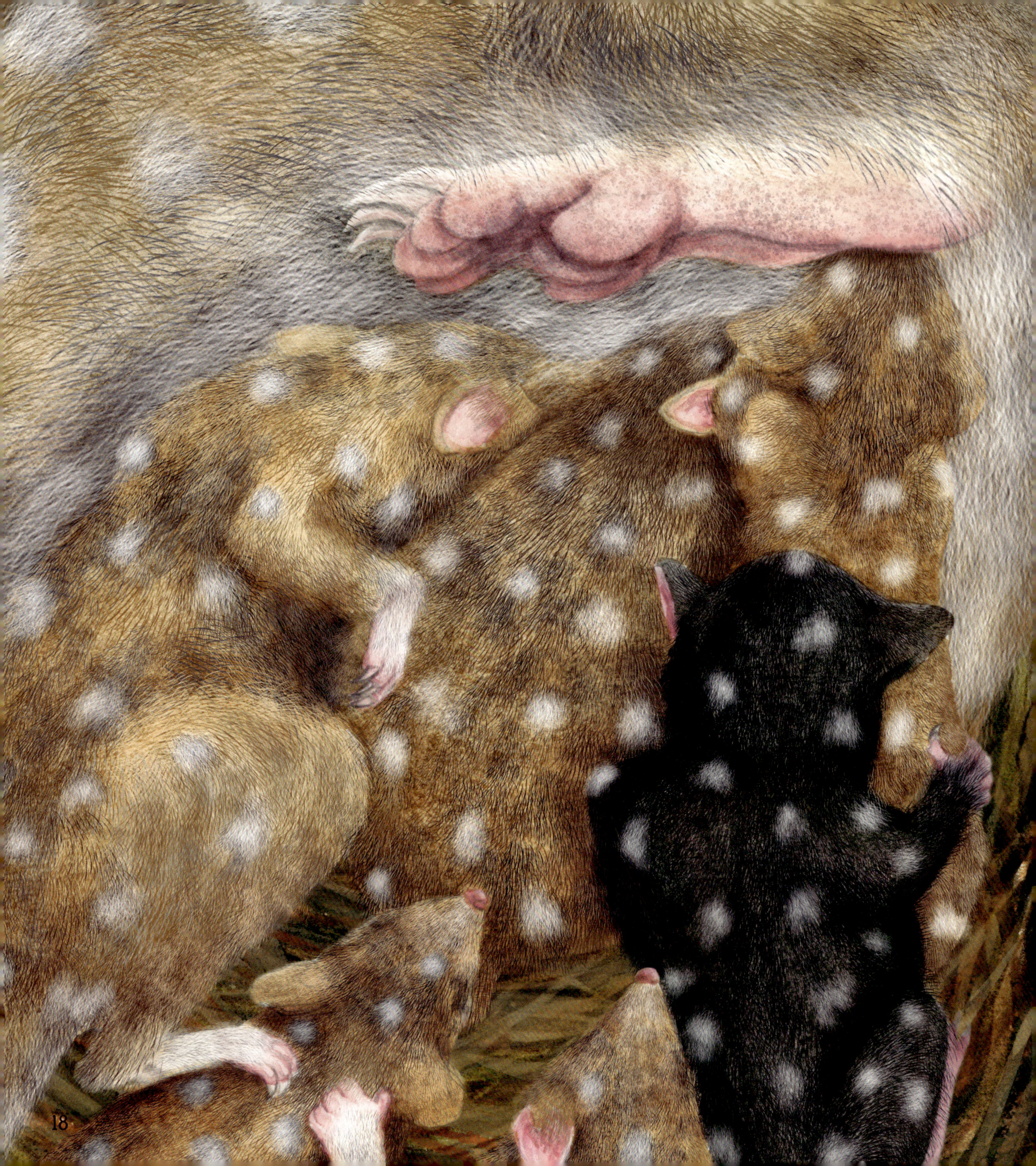

But the youngsters are hungry still. They latch on to their mother to fill their bellies with her nourishing milk.

And then all – mother and young – rest – for a while.

A female Eastern Quoll may share her den with other females, but not when nursing her young.

But soon, Quoll ventures out into the night, with her six playful young close behind. Some might even try to ride upon her back.

Juvenile Eastern Quolls are weaned when they are about five months old and gradually become independent.

The young don't stray far from their mother but they tumble off mounds, trip over branches, clamber up rock piles.

All the games they once practised inside the den, they now play outside.

They learn to scratch.

They learn to catch.

They learn to play.

They learn to hunt for food.

Male and females can breed for several years but most breeding adults are the young from the previous year.

At 15 weeks the young Eastern Quoll can catch and eat its own prey.

Mother scampers off with her young close behind. They like this game. Quoll pounces on a large bird. It will help feed hungry mouths.

Every night, they leave the den – playing games and searching for food. Travelling further through the forests. They must be alert. Young Quolls make a delicious meal for a Masked Owl.

Many Eastern Quolls do not survive past the first 6 months of independent life.

Summer is here. The young quolls will not return to their mother or the den.

They will venture across the fields. Some will find their own dens, make their own nests, and start their own brood.

Some will fall victim to other hunters.

Eastern Quolls can live in the wild for up to 4 years.

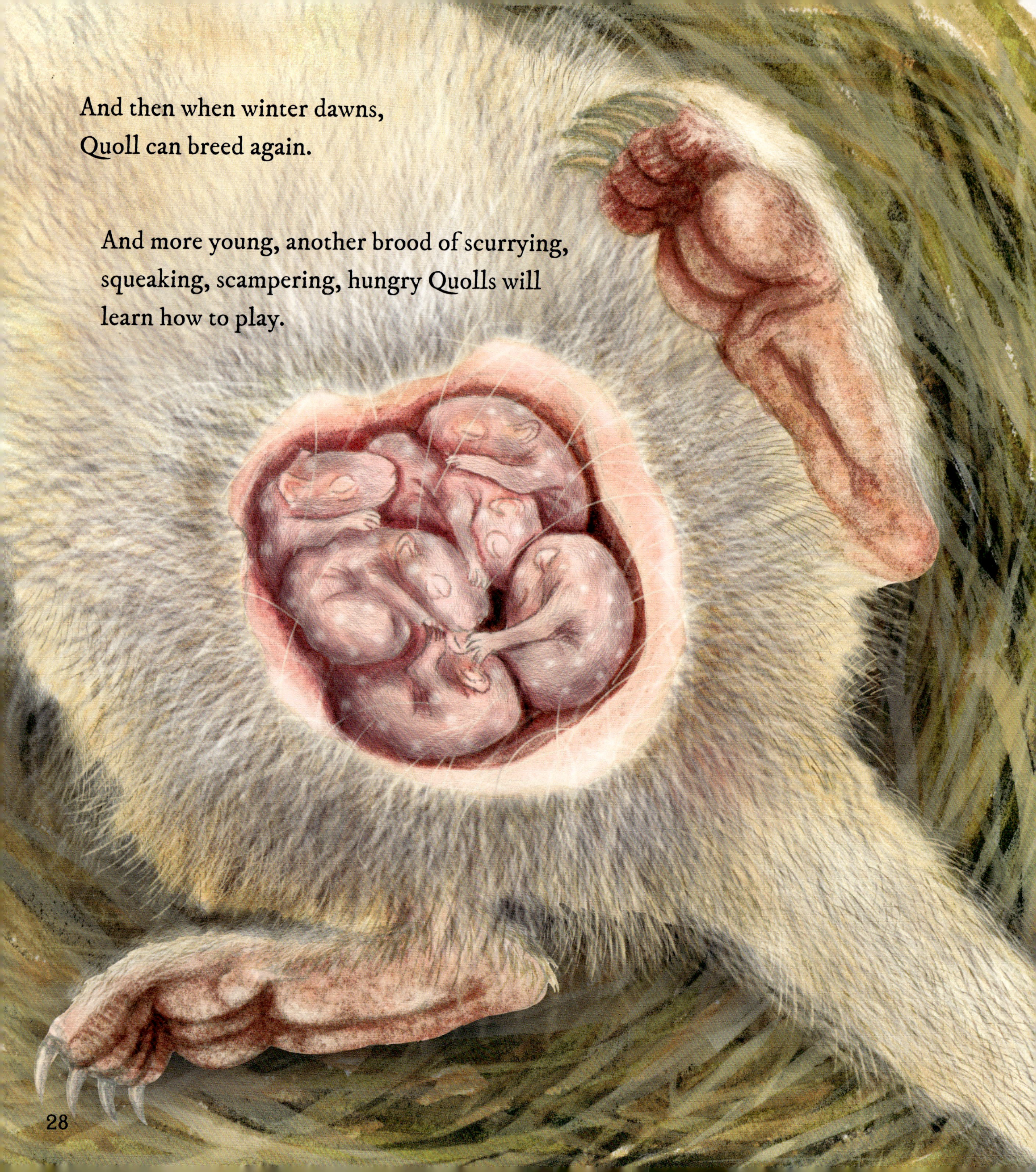

And then when winter dawns,
Quoll can breed again.

And more young, another brood of scurrying, squeaking, scampering, hungry Quolls will learn how to play.

Up to 30 undeveloped young, the size of a grain of rice, will be born ...

but only the strongest will crawl to the pouch

and latch onto one of 6 teats and continue to develop.

Information about the Eastern Quoll

The soft thick fur of the Eastern Quoll can be fawn or black and both can be in the same litter. Their body is covered in white spots but not the tail which might be white tipped and is two-thirds of its body length. Quolls are marsupials – their young are born undeveloped and then continue growing in their mothers' pouches. Once common on SE mainland Australia and Tasmania these marsupials are now only found in the wild in Tasmania having been driven to possible extinction on the mainland although successful captive breeding colonies have been established in a number of native animal sanctuaries on the mainland.

Index

Look up the pages to find out about all these quoll things.

Don't forget to look at both kinds of word – **this kind** and **this kind**.

About the author

Within the old (and new) walls of an inner-city Sydney terrace dwells Christopher Cheng. He is the author of many children's books including his previous Nature storybook title *Python* (illus. Mark Jackson) which was shortlisted for the 2013 Children's Book Council of Australia Book of the Year awards. Passionate about animals, particularly those native to Australia, it's fitting that he established the Zoomobile and taught at Taronga Zoo in Sydney for many years, celebrating his background in education.

He has always loved to write (he mostly always carries his notebook and pens) but he never thought he would be a full-time children's author.

About the illustrator

Cindy Lane grew up peering into rockpools on the northern beaches of Sydney, and not much has changed, although now it's the rockpools of sunny Perth. She illustrated her first picture book in Year 3, with her best friend as author. Cindy spends most of her time in her seaside studio, creating illustrations with a variety of paints, pigments and things she finds. She feels like a new adventure is about to happen every time she walks through the studio door!

You can watch Cindy creating at *www.instagram.com/cindylaneart*

For Hammo (and Monty, Corky, Zooma, Ding and other passengers) –
TZ was awesome. – C.C.

For all those who wonder if they can make a difference, YES you can! – C.L.

Quoll
first published in 2025
by Walker Books Australia Pty Ltd
Gadigal and Wangal Country
Locked Bag 22, Newtown
NSW 2042 Australia
www.walkerbooks.com.au

Walker Books Australia acknowledges the Traditional Owners of the country on which we work, the Gadigal and Wangal peoples of the Eora Nation, and recognises their continuing connection to the land, waters and culture. We pay our respect to their Elders past and present.

A catalogue record for this book is available from the National Library of Australia

ISBN: 978 1 760655 67 9

The illustrations in this book were created with a combination of waters and found natural pigments collected from Tasmania (with permission), watercolours, pencil, pastel, digital drawing and digital collage.
Typeset in IM Fell DW Pica and Brandon Grotesque
Printed and bound in China

EU Authorized Representative: HackettFlynn Ltd,
36 Cloch Choirneal, Balrothery, Co. Dublin, K32 C942, Ireland.
EU@walkerpublishinggroup.com

10 9 8 7 6 5 4 3 2 1

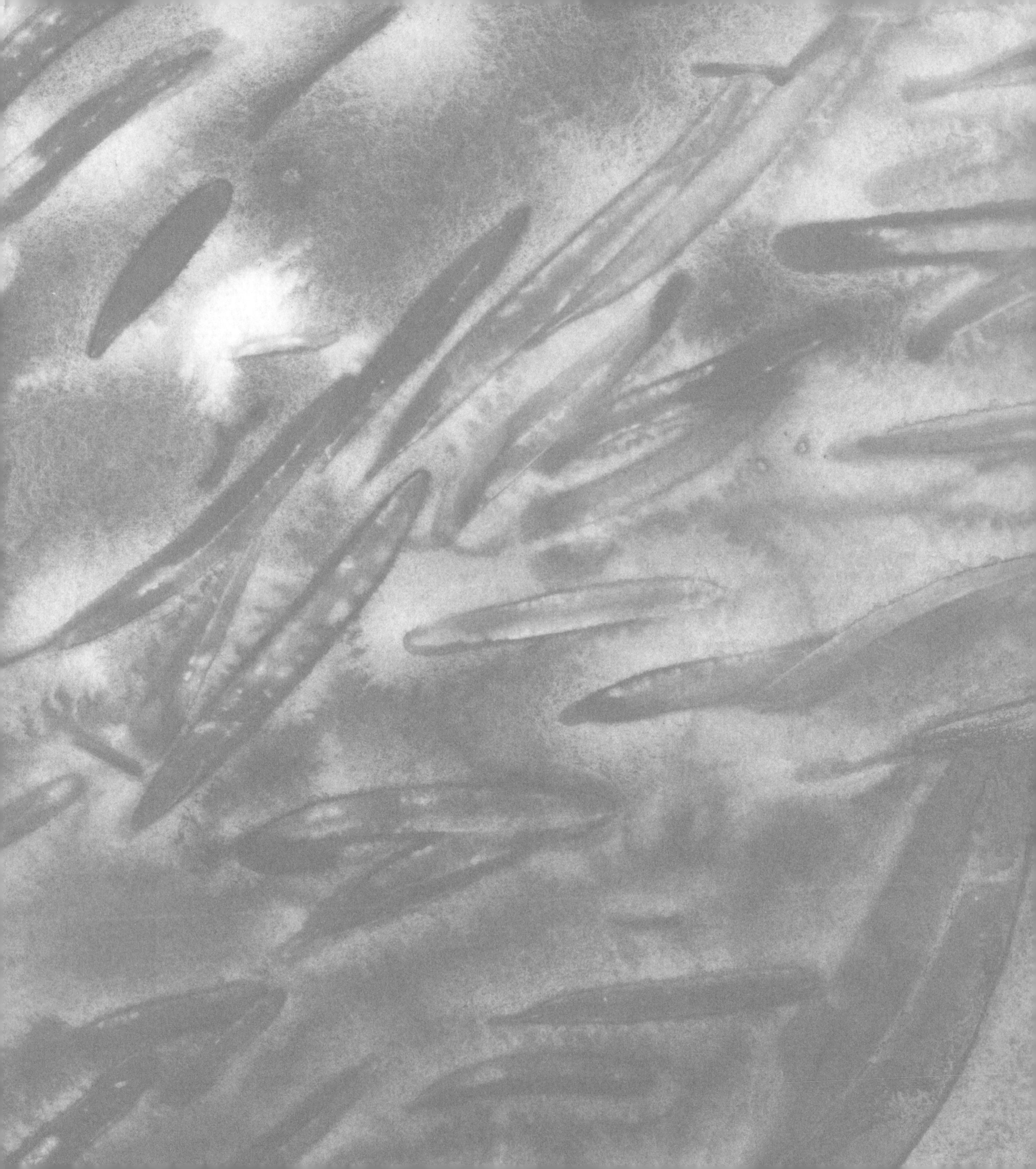